W9-AWD-686

DISCOVERING Pompeii

by Linda Cernak

Table of Contents

Introduction

The place is Italy, thousands of years ago. A small city named Pompeii bustles with activity. People go about their daily jobs. Merchants sell goods. Bakers make bread. Soldiers practice with their swords. Potters make clay pots. Girls and boys run about, playing games.

The center of town, called the forum, is a meeting place. Today it is full of people. Some visit. Some talk about making new laws. Others argue. Carts rumble through the streets beside sheep and other animals. It is a normal day in Pompeii.

The people in the town have no idea that something terrible is about to happen. Their town was built near a mountain named Vesuvius. Inside this mountain is a **volcano**.

The people in Pompeii do not know that Vesuvius will **erupt** soon. They do not know that steam, ash, and rock will suddenly spout out of an opening in the mountain and change their world.

↻ The forum was a place where people gathered daily to shop or meet with friends.

CHAPTER 1
Vesuvius Erupts

Around lunchtime, the people of Pompeii heard a loud noise. The ground shook. The top of Vesuvius had blown off! Dark, dusty **ash** and rocks shot upward into the air.

People stopped what they were doing. Bakers left bread baking in their ovens. Merchants left their goods. People began to run in fear. Some ran toward the harbor, hoping to get away by boat. Others stopped to gather money or jewelry to take with them.

↻ A cloud of burning ash, rock, and dust spread out from Vesuvius.

How Does a Volcano Form?

A volcano is formed by hot melted rock. Volcanoes erupt when pressure builds inside the earth. Melted rock called magma flows up through a vent to the earth's surface. Then it flows as lava out of the volcano. Ash and dust blow out of the volcano too.

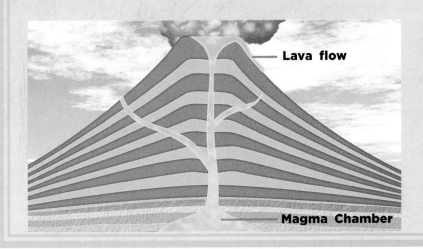

Lava flow

Magma Chamber

Many people stayed inside their houses, thinking that they would be safe. Roofs of buildings began to cave in. Others stumbled about in the darkness through the ash and rock on the streets. Wind began to blow ash and rocks over the town. The sky became dark. For hours, the ash and rock poured down on the city. Soon, Pompeii was covered in layers of ash.

↻ Some people tried to flee the city of Pompeii by boat.

People trapped beneath the ashes could not breathe. At the harbor, ash and rock fell into the sea. Huge waves crashed upon the shore. Most of the people who tried to escape by boat did not survive.

As the day wore on, the ash and rock fell on the slopes of Mount Vesuvius. It gathered in huge mounds. The next morning, the rock and ash began to flow toward the city. Soon, it hit like a giant wave. The people who were still there were buried alive.

The sky remained dark for days. Pompeii was buried under eight to ten feet of ash and rock. Only the tops of some buildings could be seen. People who had escaped came back to search through the rubble and find their homes.

Over time, people stopped searching for their homes. Pompeii became a forgotten city, lost in ash and rock.

Pliny the Younger

From the harbor, a young man named Pliny the Younger watched the volcano erupt. He wrote letters that told of what happened.

"... on Mount Vesuvius broad sheets of fire and leaping flames blazed ... the buildings were now shaking with violent shocks, and seemed to be swaying to and fro ... Ashes were already falling ... I looked round: a dense black cloud was coming up behind us ..."

CHAPTER 2
Uncovering Pompeii

Hundreds of years passed. The whole city of Pompeii was now covered with **debris**. People never guessed that a lost city was buried near the smoking volcano.

In 1710, a well digger stumbled upon the remains of a building in a nearby town. Soon people began to realize that this was the ancient city of Pompeii. Explorers and scientists began to dig up the lost city. As they inspected the ruins, they found vases, statues, and parts of homes. The digging went on for the next one hundred years, but it was not well organized. Robbers began to **loot** the buried treasures and art of Pompeii.

☝ This is a photograph of the ruins of Pompeii today. In the background you can see Mount Vesuvius.

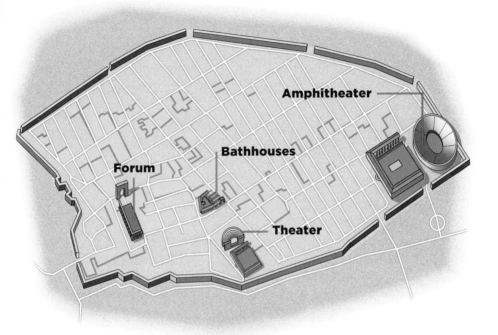

↷ This diagram shows the location of important buildings in Pompeii.

In the 1850s an Italian man named Giuseppe Fiorelli came up with a plan to uncover the city. He had the streets cleared of piles of dirt. He divided the city into sections and labeled all the houses. He stopped robbers from stealing art and treasures.

Slowly the city of Pompeii began to take shape. Fiorelli left things the way that they were when the volcano erupted. Homes, shops, and bakeries were uncovered one by one.

⋔ These plaster casts show where some victims of the disaster died.

Then Fiorelli did an amazing thing. He realized that many people died under the ash that covered the city. Over time the people's remains had rotted away. Now there was hollow space where there had once been people. Fiorelli poured plaster into the hollow spaces. The plaster filled the space and hardened. Then the ash around the plaster was chipped away.

The plaster formed the shapes of people and animals as they were when they died. It showed the looks of terror on people's faces. It was as if they had been frozen in time.

More and more of Pompeii was uncovered. Workers found homes filled with furniture and food on the tables. They found colorful mosaics, pictures made from small pieces of tile. Statues, tools, swords, cooking pots, and jewelry were left in place.

Other buildings were discovered too. The workers found a huge outdoor theater, the city's forum, and public bathhouses. All of these told the story of how people lived in Pompeii two thousand years earlier.

Making a Mosaic

Mosaics are made from tiny pieces of tile, stone, or glass. The pieces are pressed into wet plaster to form a picture. The people of Pompeii loved mosaics. Many of these works of art were found in their homes. Some people think this mosaic was the finest one found in Pompeii.

Chapter 3

Living in Ancient Pompeii

Paleontologists dug deep into the city of Pompeii to study the fossils they found there. **Archaeologists** studied buildings, tools, and other objects. These professionals began to wonder about the people of the city. How did they make their living? What were their hobbies? What games did they play?

They learned that Pompeii had been a busy city. Thousands of families lived there. There were glassblowers, potters, and bakers. Some people fished or traded goods. Nearby people worked as farmers.

Bakeries like this one were common in Pompeii.

Gladiators

Some slaves and criminals were chosen to be gladiators. They fought each other in large open theaters. Audiences loved to watch the gladiators fight with swords and daggers. Sometimes they fought animals. Many gladiators were killed during these games.

An arena in Pompeii

The city was set up in blocks, similar to some of today's neighborhoods. Gardens and fountains were everywhere. Theaters had stages for plays, speeches, and music concerts. The large outdoor theater held over 20,000 people. Fruits, spices, and fish were sold in markets.

⌒ This was probably the home of a rich person in Pompeii.

Many homes in Pompeii were found in perfect shape. Rich people often lived in homes that had kitchens, dining rooms, and bedrooms. A kitchen had a hearth, an oven, and a sink. The center of the home was often a covered courtyard. This was decorated with beautiful paintings and furniture. Poor people often lived above the shops or in small apartments.

The people of ancient Pompeii did many things in their free time. Most people went to public bathhouses. There, they could play games, swim, exercise, and bathe. Toys such as marbles, dice, dolls, tops, and hoops have been found in Pompeii too.

Schooling was important for the children of the rich. Boys were tutored by slaves or went to school. Some girls went to school, but most learned sewing and cooking. Poor children did not have an easy life. They had to work hard, like their parents.

What Did People Eat?

Many preserved foods were found at Pompeii. The people ate bread, eggs, and fish. Animal bones showed that people might have eaten the meat of sheep, cattle, and pigs. Nuts, dates, figs, and olives were other foods that people ate.

These pots were left on ➲ top of this kitchen stove by the owner.

Chapter 4
Pompeii Today– A View of the Past

Pompeii was once a beautiful, lively place filled with people. Then in one awful moment, it became frozen for all time.

Today the city of Pompeii is very much alive. You can see the remains of homes, the forum, the large theaters, and fountains. Many of these buildings stand as they did thousands of years ago.

⟳ Even this dog could not escape the dust and ash of the volcano.

⌒ We learn about life in Pompeii by looking at the art. This wall painting shows a feast.

⌒ This archaeologist works at the ruins of Pompeii.

You can also see the plaster forms of the people frozen in living positions. A woman clutches a baby. A man sits with his arms over his head. Two people hold each other for comfort.

You can now walk through the narrow streets of Pompeii. So far, over 70 homes have been uncovered. Many people's names are on their homes. Beautiful art can still be seen on the walls.

Workers still dig among the ruins of the city. They hope to find more clues buried deep in the city streets. By studying the homes, art, and objects of the past, we can learn about how people lived and what they were like.

Visitors come from all over the world to see Pompeii. The city is an outdoor museum that lets us look two thousand years into the past.

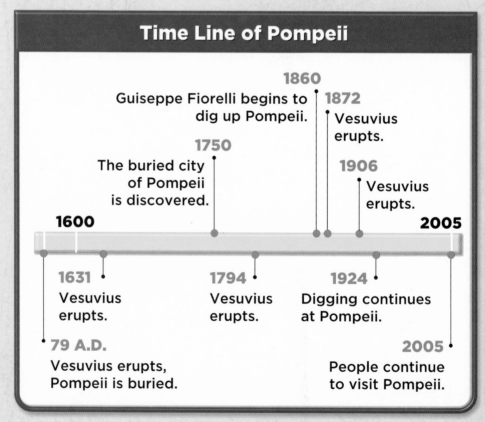

Time Line of Pompeii

1860
Guiseppe Fiorelli begins to dig up Pompeii.

1872
Vesuvius erupts.

1750
The buried city of Pompeii is discovered.

1906
Vesuvius erupts.

1600

2005

1631
Vesuvius erupts.

1794
Vesuvius erupts.

1924
Digging continues at Pompeii.

79 A.D.
Vesuvius erupts, Pompeii is buried.

2005
People continue to visit Pompeii.

Glossary

archaeologist *(ahr-kee-OL-uh-jist)* a scientist who digs up and studies the tools, weapons, and pottery of ancient cities and towns *(page 12)*

ash *(ASH)* the dust and soot from a volcano *(page 4)*

debris *(duh-BREE)* the remains of something broken down or destroyed *(page 8)*

erupt *(i-RUPT)* to break out suddenly and with force *(page 3)*

loot *(LEWT)* to steal or rob *(page 8)*

paleontologist *(pay-lee-uhn-TOL-uh-jist)* a scientist who studies fossils of prehistoric animals and plant life *(page 12)*

volcano *(vol-KAY-noh)* an opening in the surface of the earth through which lava, gas, and ash are forced out *(page 3)*

Index

Comprehension Check

Summarize

Make a list of important events and details about Pompeii. Then use the list to summarize the information in this book.

Think and Compare

1. Read pages 13 and 14. In what ways was life in Pompeii similar to or different from city life today? *(Make Generalizations)*

2. Would you like to visit the uncovered city of Pompeii? What would you like to see the most? Why? *(Apply)*

3. Why is it valuable to study the homes, tools, and art of Pompeii? *(Evaluate)*